I0134611

Squish Creativity Like a Bug

Or Lead Your Team from Ordinary to Extraordinary

By Richard M. Highsmith

Richard M. Highsmith

ISBN: 978-0615525259

To Donna whose support has been
a constant in my life
for over 35 years

The critics agree "Squish Creativity Like a Bug" is Richard's best (and only) book so far.

"A new business Guru takes center stage."
- The Chicago Tribunal

"Soon to be on our best seller list."
- The New York Thymes

"Pulitzer material…"
- The Washington Post (Office)

"I can't believe how much Ricky looks like his uncle Charlie."
- The Unadilla Tattler

"If we had excerpts to publish we might still be in business."
- Rocky Mountain News

"A must read for everyone in and out of heightened consciousness."
- The Dharma Digest

OK, OK that was all FICTION. But here are non-fiction comments by a few people I respect.

"Rick Highsmith's book may be called 'Squish Creativity Like A Bug', but the inventiveness and sense of humor that permeate the book show that Highsmith's creativity is absolutely unsquishable. A delightful read filled with great insights — particularly for those able to really see what's in the mirror."

- **Steven Cohen**, Author, "Negotiating Skills for Managers"

"Just at the time when business needs a shot in the arm, Rick delivers a brilliant and funny testament to the power of creativity that is well worth reading!"

- **Dr. John Curtis**, Author, "The Business of Love"

"This very funny book makes the management tools Rick covers very easy to understand and implement. You will learn to increase productivity and employee morale while laughing."

- **Patrick Haggerty**, Author, "Winning in the Office and on the Golf Course"

Acknowledgements

STOP & READ. This is a part of most books I skip right over. I hope you take a moment to learn writing a book isn't a solitary experience. In fact as over-worked as this sounds, I couldn't have completed this without the help of many people.

First my wife, Donna, who encouraged me to continue when I wanted to quit, who listened to some stupid ideas without snorting derisively, and who laughed when she was supposed to. She also rewrote enough material to warrant a co-authorship.

Next I want to thank my colleagues at The Leader's Institute, Doug, Craig, Rob and Frank, who helped me take the first few steps in turning a speech in to this book. Many friends and family supplied case study material. I accept complete responsibility for the changes to make them anonymous. In doing so I hope I left their thoughts and feelings intact.

I particularly appreciate Connie Timpson, my editor, who believed in the concept and helped make it happen.

And finally to all the little people...

Part One

Squish Creativity Like a Bug

By: Richard M. Highsmith

Richard M. Highsmith

Author's note: Part One is written from the point of view of the fictitious character "Mr. Steele Steadiman." You probably have worked for someone similar to him at some point in your career. If you are really unfortunate, you may work for him now. And if you are sometimes clueless as to how the world should work, you may recognize some of him in yourself. If you begin to find yourself cheering for Mr. Steadiman, please stop reading Part One of this book. Really. There is nothing new here for you to learn. To these people, I recommend you proceed to Part Two of this book.

I now give you the misinformed yet sincere Steele Steadiman...

1

Creativity is Dangerous.

"Creativity is a drug..."
                    Cecil B. DeMille

My name is Steele Steadiman and I am a Boss. If you are reading this book, you are a Boss too, or a boss wannabee. We're not "leaders" and we're not "managers." We are Bosses. Let's look at the American Heritage Dictionary definitions:

Leader: *One that leads or guides.*

Manager: *One who is in charge of business affairs.*

<u>Boss</u>: *One who makes decisions or exercises authority.*

Now I ask you. Do you want to be a "guide" or in "charge of affairs"? I didn't think so. You want to be the one who makes decisions and exercises <u>authority</u>! We all want to be Bosses because "BOSSES" are:

Beings
Of
Superior
Skills
Ego
Self-esteem

As a Being of Superior Skills, Ego and Self-esteem, you know exactly what got you to the high position you possess. The purpose of this book is to help you keep what you have earned and undoubtedly deserve. I will present key elements or rules that will allow you to be The Boss...the best boss you <u>can</u> be... the best boss you've always <u>wanted</u> to be. So pay close attention and practice, practice, practice. To begin, repeat with me:

"I am the Boss."

"I am the BOSS."

"I AM the BOSS!"

"I AM THE BOSS!!"

Doesn't that have a nice ring to it?

Now that we have established who we are, let's clarify who the enemy is. There is within your organization, oh yes, an insidious bug that eats into the natural order. It can wreck careful plans and time-honored traditions. And when you're the Boss, it's particularly detrimental. The enemy is Creativity and **Creativity is dangerous!**

Let me give you an example from my own life. I set the due date for the birth of my son for a Friday afternoon. Delivery should begin shortly after 5pm. This would allow me the weekend to execute my home management plan. I would reorganize our house, write up the rules, and integrate the baby into

the system. I could be the first to unlock my office door just like every Monday. I had a plan.

But no! Clover, my wife, always the renegade, allowed her water to break six weeks early... on a Monday! It was necessary for me to leave work and listen to an overly-cautious obstetrician go off-plan and hospitalize her until labor started. He couldn't even tell me when that would happen!

Two days later, at 3 a.m. Wednesday morning the phone blasted me from dreams of superiority. Labor had begun. In a drowsy stupor, I drove to the hospital, parked in the mostly empty garage and stumbled up to my wife's room. It was vacant. When I found the head nurse, she told me Clover had been transferred to another hospital because it was better equipped to deal with premature births. This showed a complete lack of proper planning. My wife should have been moved at a decent hour in anticipation of labor.

I drove as fast as I could to the other hospital, pulled into the garage, and then spent about 15 minutes trying to park and find my way to the entrance. The signage was very poorly designed. Some creative type had used colors rather than numbers to guide visitors! At the reception area I was informed no one with the last name of Steadiman had been admitted.

I walked the halls, looked for "Delivery Room" signs, found none, and   finally had to ask for directions. When I finally located Clover, I was immediately sent in to the bathroom to disinfect and don my sterile scrubs, mask and booties. When I came out... the room was empty. Clover was gone... again!

I sat down thinking how my plan was failing due to an excess of caution, inadequate facilities, poor architectural   design   and   administrative

incompetence.   Fifteen minutes later a nurse with a haughty attitude came in and asked me, "Why aren't you in the delivery room? Don't you want to attend the birth" *(Of course! Why else would I have sat through that bloody video on the "beauty of natural childbirth"?)* I was then hustled into the delivery room prepared to assume my role as coach for my son's birth. *(Finally, we were back on plan.)*

I got my wife's breathing under control and then contractions started. I placed my hand on her shoulder to get her attention and told her to start taking short quick breaths. She slapped my hand away and screamed, "Shut up and get the hell out of the way. I can't see the clock!" When that contraction was finished, I tried to reassume my coaching role. Clover sneered and said to me, "Do NOT interrupt my concentration by speaking or touching me again!"

With my plans in shambles I moved to the sidelines. I had to witness my son's birth as a passive observer.

While I had made excellent plans, the creativity of my son, my wife and the nursing staff had shown total disregard for the perfect plan I had created. I missed work the entire balance of the week. I might as well have yanked out all of my calendar pages for the month of May and crumpled them up! My plan had been crushed.

Trust me when I say, this same erosion of authority can, and often will, occur at work. Creativity in all its' corrupting forms can pull the rug out from under you if you don't **SQUISH IT LIKE A BUG!**

To be a stronger Boss remember:
"Creativity is Dangerous!"

Action Points:

- Remember you are a Being Of Superior Skills, Ego and Self-esteem.
- Never think of yourself as a manager or leader.
- Squish creativity whenever it confronts you.
- Repeat "I am the Boss!" often to yourself and others.

2

Fear Is The Glue That Keeps Things Running

"Men shrink less from offending one who inspires love than one who inspires fear."
Niccolo Machiavelli

When you are the Boss, you must rule with absolute authority. Keep the chokehold of control and power on your people at all times. In short, you must instill

fear in your employees. It's part of your responsibility as the Boss. Simple respect is a view or opinion of someone that is subject to change. Fear, on the other hand, is dynamic and lasting. Once someone fears you, they will most likely always fear you. As Machiavelli notes, people will shrink from offending you. More importantly, fear generates a healthy respect for the person who produced the fear. And that person needs to be **you…the Boss.**

Remind Everyone Of Their Past Failures

Over time, the human mind tends to forget or minimize mistakes. I believe this is a basic flaw in the design of the human psyche. So, to counteract this flaw, it is your job as the Boss to remind your employees of their past failures. You must bring up these errors…these unforgivable blunders… every chance you get. This will keep your employees a bit off-balance and mentally alert for the challenges of the day.

When someone barges into your office with what he or she deems as a "bright idea", you must

immediately remind him or her of a previous screw-up. It is most effective if your voice drips with disdain and scorn. Some examples might include:

"Must I remind you about the last time you thought you had an idea for the company to consider? Your plan would have created a budgetary crisis for the entire fiscal year."

Or

"Did you learn nothing at all from the fifteen minutes I laughed at your last 'bright idea'?"

Or

"Will this 'new' idea result in any long-term Workers Compensation claims like the last time?"

Or

"Susan, Susan, Susan. When are you going to learn that you are absolutely awful at creative ideas?"

I keep an active file of my staff's mistakes so I can refer to it when necessary. I call my list "losers," which stands for **L**ist **O**f **S**tupid **ER**ror**S**. I recommend you follow my example and be sure to update your Losers' folder regularly. It should include all incidents of mistakes, missed deadlines, misconduct – real or perceived - tardiness and gossip. Always include gossip.

Never underestimate the value of the Losers file. It can offer quick reference material to help you keep your employees feeling off-balance. And having this information only a click of the computer keys away will drastically reduce the number of interruptions you will face during the workweek.

Hope springs eternal, like weeds in the crack of the sidewalk. That is the nature of the human spirit. When hope pops up (which is almost always followed by some dumb idea) you have got to **squish**

it! Remind employees of their past mistakes and failures to keep them in their place.

This process is similar to the Whack The Mole game at the county fair. The mole's heads pop out of holes, and you whack 'em with a hammer. Think of the little people in your organization as moles. When they attempt to rear their heads with ideas, whack 'em. (Only figuratively, I guess) You have the hammer of historical mistakes, so use it. You are the Boss. Sometimes you have to whack several at a time, but it is imperative to keep them down!

A Good Mood Is A Waste Of Energy

Let me tell you how I arrived at this conclusion. When I was eleven-years-old, I desperately wanted an authentic Davy Crockett coonskin cap with the striped, furry tail and the Official Davy Crockett rifle. I told my parents, and wrote a letter to Santa. We even went to the local shopping center so I could tell Santa in person.

I was polite, patient and in a really good mood. This was important. I may have been a little big for Santa's lap, but I wanted… I really, really wanted that coonskin cap and rifle. I was pretty sure Santa would bring it because I had been really good when I saw him.

Into the wee hours of the morning on Christmas, I was so excited I barely closed my eyes. I just knew the cap and rifle were under the tree waiting for me. I was in a state of euphoria. Sleep would not come, and the minutes ticked by ever so slowly. I kept imagining how great it would feel to shoot the bad guys while swishing the tail on that coonskin cap.

My Dad always insisted he go downstairs first on Christmas morning and turn on the tree lights. Then he would take a picture as my sisters and I ran into the living room with smiles and sparkling eyes. I waited and waited. It seemed like hours later when he finally told us we could come down the stairs. I remember rushing down, pushing my younger sisters

aside, nearly tripping over the dog, and racing to the tree.

But no... my Dad made us go back and come into the room again. He said I had spoiled the photograph by rushing ahead of my slowpoke sisters. My elated mood at that point was bordering on hysteria. We went back out and I pushed my sisters in front of me. Dad got his picture and I finally got to the tree.

I looked at all the packages, for **the one** with my name on it. I knew it would be a long, narrow package. When I didn't see **the package**, I thought maybe you have to put the rifle together so it's in a smaller box. I systematically ripped open each present with my name, tossed the gift aside with a mere glance and reached for the next one. When I finished opening my gifts and still found no rifle, I thought maybe Santa put the wrong name on the package. I began grabbing gifts that were the right size but had my sisters' names on them. My mood began to sour.

Finally, realization struck me. There was neither a coonskin cap nor a Davy Crockett rifle in any of the packages. I was devastated. Exhausted. Inconsolable.

So what's the point of being in a good mood? I learned at age eleven it's a waste of precious energy. If you never expect anything good, you'll never be disappointed. Use the benefit of my experience, and don't expend time or energy pretending you enjoy working with the idiots around you. Wear your bad mood proudly. It is another sign you are the Boss.

Don't Allow People To Ask Questions

Remember there are no stupid questions just stupid people. I have found an excellent technique to stop people from asking questions. When someone comes up to you with a question, you say, "What a stupid question!" If they don't get the message when

you tell them the question is stupid, attack them directly. "Look, it's more than a stupid question. You're stupid!" Only a stupid person would ask a question that is so... STUPID!" This is an unparalleled way to squish initiative and creativity.

I recently watched the president of a national sports club exhibit this skill flawlessly. His human resources department (HR) had forced him to have a workshop to brainstorm creative marketing ideas for the upcoming season. Revenue was way down due to dwindling ticket sales at the box office. And a major sponsor of the franchise had withdrawn its support. The front office personnel were divided into groups. Each group had developed its ideas to present. HR had decreed the president would give out cash prizes for the teams with the most creative ideas.

On the day of the company picnic, the president had obviously given a lot of thought about how he would handle the reward ceremony. One by one, the group leaders whose marketing ideas were not accepted were called up front before their

gathered peers. The boss told each leader in detail precisely how their group's suggestions were no good. The boss wasn't going to let those leaders be confused in to thinking that anything would change.

He publicly humiliated each of the losing team leaders. He ended each degrading comment with a laugh, encouraging everyone in attendance to laugh along with him. And since he was forced to give the prize to a group with the best ideas, he selected the group whose suggestions most approximated his own plan. His next step was pure genius. He announced, "Since this team has come up with the winning ideas and obviously bought in to the plan, it will be held responsible if the plan fails." Brilliant!

Initiative Is The Next Of Kin To Creativity

When employees are allowed too much spare time, some will begin to take initiative. Do not let this happen. Take away all "spare time." Obviously individual initiative is a real threat to Bosses. **It must be crushed**. Employees who want to go outside the box and use personal initiative create never-ending problems.

In my 20s, I was a Yeoman in the U.S. Navy. A Yeoman's job is to manage the ship's office. The first Captain I was assigned to was an Annapolis graduate. He was a confident man who commanded with quiet authority. After spending a year working for him, I was transferred to another ship.

My new Captain had been in the Navy for thirty years, promoted from the ranks of enlisted men. He was short, built like a fireplug with a fiery temper to match. And he yelled. A lot. One of my

jobs on the new ship was to type correspondence for the Captain. In one of my first assignments, I had the audacity to show initiative and correct some spelling and grammatical issues I found in his draft. After typing the letter, I left it on the desk in his stateroom.

Later, I was sitting in the ship's office reading when the bulkhead door flew open. The Captain was red-faced and highly agitated. He let me know in very colorful language that it was disrespectful for an underling to change the writings of a superior officer. He told me bluntly, "Write what I say. Exactly. Don't ever change a word." At the time, I was dumbfounded. I had no clue as to the problem I had created.

Now as a mature Boss myself I understand my Captain's rage. I recognize the danger of taking personal initiative. What if Shakespeare's scribe had edited the Bard's sentence structure? What if Moses had paraphrased God's Ten Commandments? What if a lowly painting assistant had made changes in Michelangelo's masterpiece on the Sistine Chapel

ceiling? What if a concrete pourer had altered the ratio of materials while building the Golden Gate Bridge or Hoover Dam?

The inventiveness of these "initiative takers" could have had dire consequences. Your task is clear. When an employee exhibits potentially treacherous initiative... **crush it**. You need to understand that they do not have the knowledgeable insight you possess. Use all of your authority to demand absolute compliance.

To be a stronger Boss remember:
"Fear Is The Glue That
Keeps Things Running"

Action Points

- Rule the future by bringing up past failures.
- Don't waste energy on a good mood.
- Discourage or stomp on people's questions.
- Crush initiative. It is the kissing cousin of creativity.

3

Never Acknowledge The Importance Of The People Who Work For You

"I am not sure that it is of the first importance that you should be happy. Many an unhappy man has been of deep service to himself and to the world."

Woodrow Wilson

You are the Boss. And the Boss has the responsibility to make sure everything and everyone

works. You know where things belong and how your people are supposed to accomplish the business objectives. Do they need to be happy while following your orders? President Wilson was right. The only possible answer to this question is NO!

You Are The One With The Big Picture

The little people working for you should focus on their small piece of the workplace. They don't have the capacity to look beyond what's right in front of them. There are many examples of this throughout history.

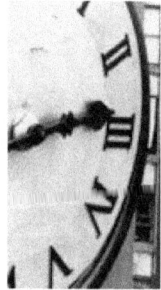

When Alexander Graham Bell placed the world's first phone call to Mr. Watson, the phone rang, Watson answered, and simply brought Bell a rag. Watson didn't realize he was the first person to ever receive a telephone call. And... he did not need to know.

Andrew Mellon, Secretary of the Treasury, told President Herbert Hoover the economy was fine in

1929. He had money in **his** checking account.

Bosses have an exalted vista the peons cannot

see. Dan Quayle (one of my heroes) once said, *"The global importance of the Middle East is that it keeps the Far East and the Near East from encroaching on each other."* That is what understanding the Big Picture means.

When one of your peons stumbles across a good idea, immediately take credit. It's part of your big picture view. Take credit for all creative thinking and problem solving. This is your role. Protect your subordinates from the scrutiny of top management by never conceding the part they play in your successes. Your people take pride in serving you and feeding you their good ideas. Your bright light is enough to keep them tanned.

Remember you're the Boss and they are your supporting cast. When you go to a Clint Eastwood movie, his name comes before the title... like CLINT EASTWOOD in "Million Dollar Baby." He starred in it. He directed it. What more do we need to know? If you insist on learning the names of the commoners who helped make the movie, you have to wait until the end-credits. And, really, who has enough popcorn or interest to stay for the credits?!

The little people like Morgan Freeman or Hillary Swank might get a little attention. But who cares about the author of the book? Without Clint the book would have collected dust on a library shelf. He made it a big deal. He saw the big picture. (As an historical footnote, you should know a HR egghead invented end-credits.)

Remind your employees they are not associates or partners. They get a paycheck to do their job. If you praise an employee for one good idea, he or she will come up with ninety-nine bad ones and they <u>will</u>

keep bothering you. So don't allow their bad ideas to waste your valuable time. Speak for your staff. Follow the chain of command. Claim the credit. You deserve it! You're the boss.

Nobody Likes Cheerleaders
(Except Maybe The Football Players)

Remember the cheerleaders back in high school? Stuck up skinny girls who thought they were better than everybody else. My personal insight and experience is that nobody really liked the cheerleaders. Who can stand all those smiles with the glint of white teeth?

I never dated a cheerleader. I had important things on my mind. Besides, none of them would talk to me. And who cared? I had the big picture. There was one little downside. You had to act like you liked the cheerleaders. If you didn't, a couple of unhappy words from the "rah rah girls" could cost you a black eye – courtesy of their football boyfriends.

It is the same at work. Nobody respects a boss who goes around saying, "Rah, Rah, Rah. Go team!"

Work should be... well... work! I do not care if the employees like it or not. In fact, I believe "rah rah" leads to "blah blah." If you're always going around trying to build morale, saying silly things like, "Good job," employees will try harder and expect more. Soon they'll think you approve of them and that will inevitably lead them to suggest ideas they believe will "improve" the workplace. Now you will have a group of scatterbrained nobodies thinking independently and undermining your authority as the Boss.

You don't want that and **your** Boss doesn't want that. The last thing you both need is your people going to the big Boss with their harebrained ideas about how to improve the company. You are the boss. Keep the morale low. Hope and creative thinking will soon become nothing more than a dumb

idea they had when they were kids. They were lucky it did not blow the house up. Low morale breeds low expectations and makes your job as the boss a lot easier.

The Pay is the Thing

Every year The American Management Association (AMA) aggravates me by investigating why people leave jobs. Topping their "whiner's" list is, "relationship with my manager." Why don't they get it? We are bosses not managers? Right there their "stupid survey" is flawed. They didn't even use the right terminology. I would never belong to AMA because it has the word "management" in it. "Relationship with my Manager?" - I got no relationship with the people who work for me, and I pride myself in not wanting a relationship with people at work. We all know people work for the paycheck. If I did not pay my people they would stop rushing from the elevator to beat the time clock.

(And that can be funny because they know I will dock their pay if they are more than two minutes late.) They would stop showing up at all if they did not get a check. It is obvious that those "always in favor of the worker" HR people did this study. They told people taking the survey to check pay as fourth or fifth most important. Showing pay as anything but number one is crazy. The pay is the thing because if you don't pay people, they are not going to come to work.

The AMA can say whatever they want about relationships and touchy-feely stuff, but they have disregarded the basic rule of work, "no pay – no show." The pay is enough incentive for employees to keep plugging their card into the magic work machine. I don't need to go to all the trouble and all the hassle of running around praising people, acknowledging people, and all that stuff, when I do not mean it anyway. I'm the boss. I get the praise. They get a paycheck and that's enough expression of the company's appreciation. Pay is all they should get for doing their job.

Tried And True Is Right For You

That has a nice ring to it, doesn't it? As the Boss, you do not want to try new, innovative creative things. You got to be the Boss because you do things a certain way. Your methods, your style, your path is time tested and proven in many situations and circumstances. It is the well-traveled path, the comfortable path. You will not trip on unexpected rocks in the road; it minimizes surprises and nearly eliminates change.

Let's look at the once giant Kmart as an example of "taking the path not proven", trying to make changes that lead to colossal failure. The spoiler, Wal-Mart, was gaining market share. Instead of focusing on delivering quality products at great prices, Kmart tried to move up and speed down a new path to compete with Target.

Kmart moved on a huge deal, signing that crafty, creative, Martha Stewart. And we all know where she moved next, trendy ankle bracelet and all. Think monochrome gray-green wall colors with low, low, thread-count linens.

Kmart stopped doing what they knew best and tried change. Now, in what some financial wizards are calling a mega-failure, Kmart is part of Sears. (I like to call it the "Mega-Martha, way too creative" Kmart failure.) This is a clear lesson for management guru's who advocate the importance of change. I'm sure there are many bosses at what's left of Kmart who wish the company had stuck to tried and true.

You don't want to change minor things either. You don't have to, because you're the Boss. Bob, a good friend of mine, was the Executive Director of a community services organization. With the economy tripping over rock after boulder, headed for a complete dirt dive, his agency was losing local financial support.

At first he did all the right things. He reduced staff salary (except his own), laid people off and reduced services. Then he danced with the creative devil in an effort to tap in to larger sources of funding. He held his hand out in partnership to a national organization, which provided the same type of community service. His Board of Directors supported this creative approach.

Bob was happy. There was new revenue money in his organization's account. But with the new revenue source came a demand to give up some control. As the funding grew, so did the influence the larger agency had with Bob's Board.

After several months, Bob heard whispers, and then talk. The national organization offered to merge. The Board capitulated. Board members saw this as a way to solve the financial crisis and unanimously voted in favor of the merger. The first creative action the larger organization took after the approval was to "retire" Bob!

If Bob wasn't forced to move to Boise, he could personally tell you, "Creative change, any change is dangerous!" It's scary <u>and</u> dangerous, like a runaway train. If things get changed somebody else might become the Boss. Resist change. "We've always done it that way" is more than a saying. It's a way of life!

To become a stronger Boss remember:
"Never acknowledge the importance of people who work for you."

Action Points:

- Own the Big Picture and do not share it.
- Don't be a cheerleader – Nobody likes cheerleaders except maybe football players.
- Rely on old-fashioned "pay" as a motivator.
- Live your mantra: Tried and true is right for you.

Richard M. Highsmith

4

Give Your Opinion First, Forcefully and Often

"The power of accurate observation is commonly called cynicism by those who have not got it."
George Bernard Shaw

Who knows more about running your department than you? No one. That's right. How could someone toiling in the trenches with no Big-Picture mentality possibly grasp situations and

problems as well as you? You alone have the candlepower to illuminate the dark crevices that big problems create. It is imperative for your subordinates to know where you stand. Won't they be like sailors at sea without a compass if you don't give them direction? Naturally they will turn to you for guidance. Why wait?

Give them the answers before they even know to ask the questions. No one knows more about the operation than you. And if they try to get smart and ask questions that are not on your Boss's list of questions you want to answer, just ignore them. Or tell them they do not need that information to do their little jobs. Remind them you are in control. You are the boss.

Remember You Are The **Big** Dog

You are the St. Bernard... the Great Dane. I personally like the image of the Great Dane - great size, dignity, strength - the Apollo of all breeds. (If you prefer fine wines and liquors, then the St. Bernard with the keg of aged brandy strapped to its

neck might be a better image for you.) Your employees are like Chihuahuas. While a Great Dane is regal and dignified, Chihuahuas can be pesky, ankle nipping and yippy, yapping little creatures. The Great Dane simply does not acknowledge the Chihuahuas. Nor should he. But he does know the little guys look up to him for guidance and protection.

Napoleon had the right idea. Check your history books. When confronted with a problem, General Bonaparte would figure out all the details for a successful campaign...the absolute best course of action. After all, he was the Big Dog – The Boss. Did his soldiers attempt to give him advice? I don't think so.

When your employees attempt to give their views and ideas, remember, as their leader you must strongly and expertly tell them exactly what will

happen. You've already charted the course, worked out the solution... and taken the credit. Just be honest. Tell them bluntly that their "inexperienced, naive input" confuses everyone and threatens to destroy the mission.

Do Not Ask Other People's Opinions

Do not **ever** ask a peon's opinion. I cannot stress enough just how important this directive is in your life as the Boss. Keep in mind "peon" is "PERSON" with the R & S taken out. And we all know that R & S stand for the **R**ight **S**tuff. If the individual questioning you had it, he or she wouldn't be a peon! If you remember nothing else in this book – remember this:

You do not need to, nor should you, waste your time listening to a peon's opinion.

One slip up on your part and each and every employee will begin telling you things you do not want to hear.

If you even act like you are listening they will hound you with more and more inane suggestions. Remember, they are yippy little Chihuahuas. Just wave a newspaper at them.

Employees need to be managed and kept inside the box with the lid closed, sound proofed, sealed with duct tape, and tied with twine, preferably with layers and layers of twine wrapped and tied tightly around the box. You never want them to reach outside of their boxes!

Peons should do exactly what they are paid to do and keep their mouths shut. Their role is to make *your* job function more easily. For their efforts to make your life easier, they are rewarded handsomely with a paycheck.

And don't ask questions of the peons unless it is to put them in their place, like, "Why are you talking to me?" If you start asking peons general, or pretending-to-be-nice, questions, I promise your job will become really messy. People will tell you things you do not want to hear. You will lose control of the situation and your projects will fail.

Listening Is Way Overrated

My personal approach to listening is, **I don't**. My advice to you - do not even pretend to listen. You do not have to. You are the boss.

Some people are so stupid. You can be sitting in your office busily working when an employee will take it upon himself or herself to stand in front of your desk and talk non-stop about absolutely nothing of importance to you or the work you are doing. You can keep working, paying no attention to them and somehow they will still assume you are listening to them rattle on. Sometimes rolling your eyes or sneering helps, but not usually.

In this situation... be the boss. It's for their own good. Use a little tough boss language, like "Shut up! Get out of my office. Take your inane comments with you and close the door behind you. I don't know how the door got open to begin with because my policy is **the door is always closed**."

Yes, even when you are ignoring people, if you don't make it really clear, they will continue to share their ridiculous views and opinions. If telling them to "shut up" only slows them down, attack them personally. Call them names! Let them know what you think of them. Really. (I also use this approach to stop employees from asking stupid questions.) Use words like boneheaded, dimwitted, slow, dull, brainless and annoying. These should effectively stop the interloper in his or her tracks. And you will be a

hero to your boss. You have prevented employees from wasting your precious time and hence saved your company money.

You must make your position perfectly clear at all times. If you allow one person to interrupt your important work, others will follow. So keep your door closed and go on the offensive immediately when someone violates the sanctity of your private space. Show your anger and verbally attack the trespasser.

This is a powerful technique. But be very careful. In the good old days you had a Director of Personnel to back you up. Now it has morphed into something called Human Resources. *(What is that about?!)* I say that they are eggheads who know nothing but somehow wheedled a job for themselves. The point is, they do exist. And if you go around telling too many people they are stupid, someone might rat you out to HR. Then one of the eggheads who doesn't know anything about being a Boss, will come and try to tell you how to do your job. So use

name-calling sparingly. It's a great technique, but its like cayenne pepper – a little goes a long way. Just know that you may have to swallow it!

Never Make Eye Contact

I mean it. Never, ever make eye contact, and you will be a successful boss. In fact, I believe casual eye contact sends an undesirable body language signal. When you look people in the eye while they are talking, you give the impression you are listening. (You do not want that!) Even worse, some will interpret your visual contact as interest in their babbling. So now the simple act of making eye contact has created the impression you actually care about the person speaking, and what they are talking about. Since nothing could be further from the truth, it is important to avoid the illusion.

One of my first bosses had an amazing talent. He never, ever looked into a subordinate's eyes while he or she was talking. He would mostly look out the window. But if he happened to turn his head in your

direction, he would close his eyes before he faced you. This incredible technique makes the peon feel unworthy and is a sure fire way to keep their inane comments to a minimum. No eye contact. It works beautifully.

The exception to this rule is when you are scolding an employee. Don't focus on them constantly because they become accustomed to it. Save the glare for the points you wish to underscore. In the following admonishment I have put [brackets] around the words where severe eye contact would have the best impact. *"In all my years of supervision this is the most [incompetent] handling of paperwork I have ever observed. Your [stupidity] is unfathomable. I mean really, this is so [simple] a nine-year-old wouldn't break a mental sweat. But you have managed to set a [new low in ineptitude."]*

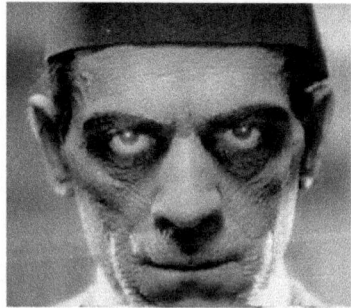

Notice how the eye contact underscores the key words. The employee receiving this dressing-down could not possibly fail to feel the full power of your authority.

To be a stronger Boss remember:
"Give your opinion first, forcefully
and often."

Action Points:

- Remember you are the Big Dog.
- Do not ask other people's opinions.
- Do not waste precious time listening.
- Never make eye contact.

5

Keep People Busy.

"Idleness is the only refuge of weak minds and the holiday for fools."

Lord Chesterfield

As the boss, you <u>never</u> want to allow anyone to stand or sit around doing nothing. Lord Chesterfield was a politician who understood business. You supervise a bunch of weak-minded fools. You need

to keep them busy between assignments. This busy work keeps them from interfering with what others are working on within your department. And as I am sure you understand by now, idle time gives employees way too much time to think up stupid new ideas or ask idiotic questions that you have no intention of answering. So crack the whip! Keep them from drifting away on a mental holiday.

Make Your Files The Bermuda Triangle

Always keep a file of your favorite personal brainstorms. When you catch someone looking idle, hand out one of your "ideas" to develop. Let them design the action steps, cost breakdowns, manpower requirements, etc. Tell them to cover all bases and contingencies. Then when they have finished, file all this information away. You

naturally have no intention of actually carrying out any of these projects. There is, however, a personal benefit. You can use these well-developed files of ideas and action steps to look important and prepared to <u>your</u> boss. The biggest benefit of all - your employees will be kept off-kilter. They'll continue to wonder: "Does this meet the Boss's standards? When are we going to begin the project? What role will I have?"

Now, the next step is very important. Without addressing the last project, give them another one of your brilliant ideas to develop. Steadfastly refuse to answer any questions regarding the previous project they slaved over. Just tell them to get it done. If you believe it will be helpful to keep morale down, you might nitpick, criticize and mislead them about the quality of the work. Say something like, *"The last project looked promising until your analysis proved nonsensical."* This approach forces them to attempt to improve the quality of their work without any real direction or sense of accomplishment.

Middle Managers Are Not Your Friends

You should be friendly and let them think they are "almost" bosses. However, do not give them a parking space, never confide in them nor treat them as equals. In fact, talk over them whenever possible. Do not trust them. Berate them and always have in the back of your mind, "They are like the next Pez candy behind me in the dispenser. They hope I will fall to the floor and break into pieces."

A superlative approach to these remoras under you is to give them titles and responsibility, but no real authority to act without your permission. I once had a Boss that executed this maneuver with exceptional aplomb. I was a newly minted supervisor. She called all of us together and directed us to come up with ideas about how to spend the advertising budget for the coming year.

I was excited. All of us spent time outside of work hours preparing to present our well-crafted

ideas. This wily boss required us to submit them in writing prior to the meeting. As we presented our ideas, she encouraged others to point out flaws and pitfalls. We spent two hours debating the advantages and disadvantages of each proposition. She skillfully guided the discussion. At one point the group was leaning toward one particular option. She asked me to summarize the positives. When I was done she stated that "obviously" this proposal was "stupid."

I was so in awe of her command of the meeting that I forgot to feel bad. Ultimately when only one option remained she allowed us to vote. She concluded by saying, *"It's a good thing you all agree because that's what I was planning to do with the advertising budget anyway."* The message was clear. I may have been called a supervisor but I was nothing next to her because she was the undisputed, undeniable Boss!

So when the "Boss wannabe's" make decisions, undercut them. Publicly point out weak-minded logic. Tell them their project is not up to the standards of the company. Blame them for anything and everything that goes wrong. I mean this literally. If sales are down, it is their fault. If a project falls behind schedule, it's their fault. If the sandwiches were delivered late, it's their fault. Whatever "wrong" happens, **it's their fault!**

Do Not Be Your Own Worst Enemy

As Bosses we know we are right. As humans we must be ever vigilant that the seeds of doubt have no opportunity to sprout. Bertrand Russell, a twentieth century philosopher said, *"The trouble with the world is that the stupid are cocksure and the intelligent are full of doubt."*

You are not stupid, so never doubt <u>yourself</u>.

Don't over-think your response to a situation. Go with your gut instinct. Never allow yourself to question any action you have taken. You did what was needed to be done. If some peon questions you

after the fact, recognize the source. You are the Boss for a reason. Your past decisions led **you** and nobody else to this position. This peon has no right to question your decision.

So keep your guard up and be ready to squish any glimmers of creativity...like a bug! (Yes even yours.) Glimmers are insidious. They act like fireflies, casting all kinds of unwanted light and energy into your pure, staid thinking. You, more than anyone else, know what it takes to be the Boss, to be right all the time. You have what it takes... the Right Stuff!

To be a stronger Boss remember:
"Keep people busy."

Action Points:

- Make your files the Bermuda Triangle.
- Ignore or intimidate middle managers.
- Do not be your own worst enemy.

6

CONCLUSION

"The life of man is of no greater importance to the universe than that of an oyster."

David Hume

Mr. Hume was of course not referring to Bosses when he penned this line. If you don't understand that yet, you should read this book again. This time pay attention. However, the sentiment certainly applies to the legions of peons who work for

us. Employees are like rooks in a chess game. Bosses use them to make strategic moves. Never mind that the move could kill the rook. They are sacrificed for the greater good. Besides, there are always others waiting to take their place. Just toss them off the board!

It has been said that among the worries of today's Bosses is the large number of unemployed still on the payroll. Pull the trigger and fire them. Turnover helps clear out the deadwood. Does it really matter who cashes the paycheck, as long as the work gets done?

With these thoughts in mind it is clear that you owe your employees nothing other than a little pay for their time. Your role is to maintain control and guide your department or company to profitability.

You do NOT need interference from creative employees.

Even the brightest and the best peons need direction and guidance. If they didn't, this book wouldn't be necessary. Very bright people with weak leaders created some of the worst foul-ups I have ever seen. There is an ancient Arabian axiom, which illuminates these points. It is my mantra and I try to live by it every day. *"An army of sheep lead by a lion will defeat an army of lions lead by a sheep."*

And so I end this guidebook on becoming a better Boss with the same words I started. Creativity is insidious and detrimental to bosses in every organization. It is up to you to **squish creativity** in all its wicked forms wherever and whenever it appears. Because... **you are the BOSS!**

Richard M. Highsmith

AFTER DINNER KEYNOTE SPEAKER

Consider a humorous, irreverent speaker for your next corporate event. Spend an hour with Rick Highsmith as Steele Steadiman. Laugh at the foibles of Steele as he expounds on his "Creativity is Dangerous" philosophy.

Rick combines over 25 years of experience as a trainer and business coach with his own improvisational comedy training to bring you this delightful "life from the trenches" monologue.

Learn more by going online to http://www.SteeleSteadiman.com

Richard M. Highsmith

Part Two

Lead Your Team from Ordinary to Extraordinary

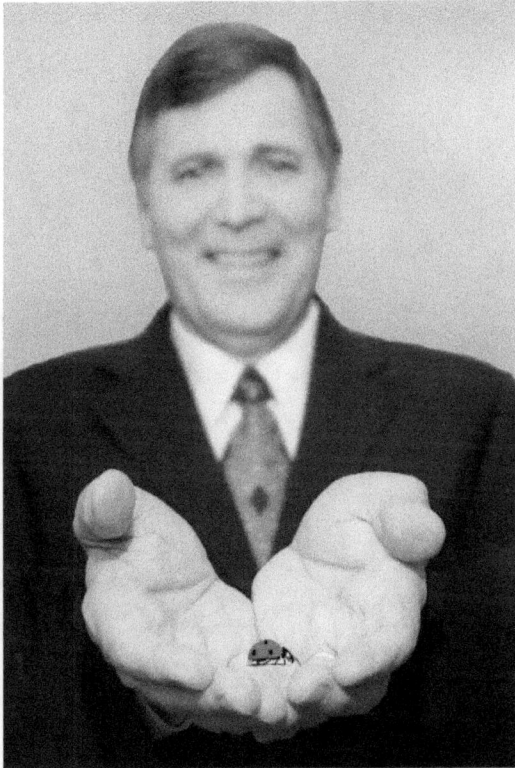

By Richard M. Highsmith

Author's note: This is Part Two of the book. If you have not read the comments of Mr. Steele Steadiman, you might want to read Part One first. If you have completed Part One and identified with Mr. Steadiman, I feel compelled to warn you this half of the book will not be fun.

1

"Steele" believes creativity is dangerous. In reality,

Creativity is Vital.

*"Creativity can solve almost any problem. The creative act,
the defeat of habit by originality, overcomes everything."*
George Lois

Highly effective managers acknowledge the importance of having the support, loyalty and ideas of their subordinates. They understand their professional success depends on it. Unfortunately bosses like Steele are all too common. They are generally clueless as to why their employees do not respect them, challenge them and sometimes refuse to comply with simple requests. They question why these employees act and seem uncaring about their job performances. Yet, these bosses rarely reflect back on their own performances as a manager, a company leader and a mentor.

The magical, entrepreneurial spark of one person can evolve into an exciting business concept when employees are allowed – nay encouraged - to soar on the wings of their own creativity. The primary role of a successful manager must be the professional development and encouragement of those who report to him or her.

The fundamental paths to success can be challenging and sometimes confusing. So just how does a manager walk through the corporate jungle and avoid **squishing creativity like a bug?**

In this part of the book we will explore real-life examples of successes in management. We'll also look at some Steele-like horror stories and show you creative ways to turn these negative situations into positive, affirming achievements. Through the behaviors of others, you can be inspired to become a successful leader and manager by liberating your own creativity.

Action Ideas – Chapter One

To fully appreciate and understand the importance of creativity:

- Forget the "rules" of Steele Steadiman.
- Understand your career success will evolve from the success of your employees.
- Embrace creativity and change.

2

"Steele" believes fear is the glue that keeps things running. In reality,

Fear destroys employee confidence.

"To live a creative life, we must lose our fear of being wrong."
Joseph Chilton Pearce

Fear of the boss, or the boss's system, destroys creativity. Fear creeps into the workplace in many ways: fear of making a mistake; fear of other peoples' opinions; fear of embarrassment; fear of change. The more afraid employees are, the less creative they will be. It is a well-accepted scientific belief that we humans need to feel secure to focus on higher-level intellectual tasks.

Let's look at examples of how managers' reactions impacted various creative problem-solving situations. I'll point out specific positive ways when managers are on top of their game. But when a manager has a misstep, I'll show you how to easily turn it around.

The first example comes from a former attendee of my management course, who was describing an early job experience. Greg was working as a forklift operator.

" I learned quickly there was no pleasing the Warehouse Manager at my new job. As a poorly skilled leader, his only tools were to intimidate and lie in an attempt to make himself look good. He never sought ideas from the crew and often his directions were wrong. If you questioned him he would get very irritated and demand strict

compliance.

I was tasked to rearrange the refrigerated storeroom. He gave me specific instructions that would have resulted in blocked inventory, too small aisles for our equipment and some overloading of pallet racks. I tried to explain the problems, but he would not listen to my ideas. I was almost done with the project when the Supervisor came in. He watched for a moment and then exploded at me, telling me all the things I had told my manager. I explained to him as calmly as I could why I was doing it wrong. He let me rearrange the room correctly.

When confronted by the Supervisor, my manager told him the original way was my idea and I had disobeyed his instructions. He then came and attacked me for "lying" to the Supervisor and not doing it "his way" in the first place. Later the Supervisor told me he was aware of the manager's behavior and not to worry about it. Unfortunately the Supervisor took no further action and I ultimately left the job because of the constant conflict."

Greg's manager was so focused on controlling his subordinates through intimidation, that he not only blocked creative solutions, but he also created chaos and conflict in the work place. When Greg overcame his fear and tried to help, by pointing out an obvious problem, he was reproached. In the end the company lost a bright young employee and very likely repeated its bad management with future hires.

The Supervisor, Greg's manager's boss, needed to become more closely involved with the manager. By addressing situations like this as they came up, the Supervisor may have been able to turn "negative behavior" into a "positive management style." Managers like this will not give up old, practiced behaviors easily. However, setting a strong positive example, using corrective counseling that focuses on specific inappropriate behavior can turn a negative incident and style into a positive teaching opportunity. The result is a more productive and positive workplace.

My second example is from a former colleague,

Jane who is a corporate trainer.

"I worked with a woman who owned her own small organizational consulting company. I still consider her to be my mentor. She actively sought out the ideas of the trainers that worked with her and had enough wisdom and humility to understand that collaboratively we could come up with much better ideas than she could alone. Even though sometimes she made "executive decisions," this was the exception rather than the rule. Once, when I told her she was my mentor she said, "I don't want to be anyone's mentor; we're a team here and you teach me as much as I teach you." She's the best boss I've ever had precisely because she wouldn't want to be called that!"

Jane's mentor believed all employees were valuable storehouses of information. She tapped in to that source by creating a safe environment where her employees did not feel threatened or vulnerable when offering ideas. The result was a dynamic team that felt self-assured and comfortable offering ideas.

Richard M. Highsmith

A skilled leader has no ego when it comes to problem solving or finding new ideas. So why do we so seldom see this kind of leadership? It comes down to each individual manager, his or her temperament, experience, and personality.

We are taught early in life that the tough competitor gets the spotlight. And there are some managers who use intimidation and fear to turn down the wattage on their employees, keeping the bright light focused on themselves. However, an effective, creative manager puts the spotlight on the individual who came up with the "bright idea" or exhibited positive behavior. When I solicited case studies from friends, colleagues and family, "management by fear" and "light-stealing management" were described more than any other styles. These are commonly experienced by employees and not easily forgotten. I chose the next three examples to illustrate these problems. Following the examples, I will explain what a good manager should do.

First, Carolyn, a colleague who formerly worked at a marketing company told me about what it was like to work for a creative genius.

"When a guy builds a concept from a garage business to a $40 million dollar company, he's certainly got some talent. Despite his genius, my former CEO had a knack for squelching creativity of any kind from his employees. He jumped to conclusions before hearing the full idea and often rejected things simply because they weren't his. His intimidating response to any idea was, "Let me tell you why that's not going to work". Marketing meetings were pretty quiet and one-directional. After telling us all his latest ideas, he would say something like, "Why do I have to come up with every campaign concept? What am I paying you people for?" We would all figuratively roll our eyes. The only variation on this theme was when a new kid was added to the team. Invariably they would try and impress everyone with their creative thoughts until they had been initiated by the CEO's complete rejection."

The second story came from my cousin, who worked for an engineering firm. Her CEO said all the right things but...

> "Our CEO would hold meetings and tell us how important we were to the success of the company and encourage us to speak openly and freely... no bad ideas, no stupid questions, blah, blah, blah. It didn't take us long to figure out he was reading from a script and didn't mean a word he was saying. As new people came on board, he would give that speech at our next monthly meeting. It became hysterical to watch these poor newbie's raise their hands to share only to be slapped down and embarrassed by the CEO.
>
> My feeling and those of my coworkers was we would have preferred being told to sit down, shut up, do your work and keep your job. Actually the offices were very nice and we were well paid. It was also an interesting social study to watch how the employees banded together on projects and presentations to deliver a great product in spite of this phony."

And, finally, an example from Ben. He still works for a security-technology company.

> *"We were experiencing some difficult times, losing market share to a competitor. A required-attendance phone conference was scheduled. The group President asked for everyone to be creative and honest to come up with ways to gain some traction in sales. The first person to speak stated a well-known fact. The competitor's product had superior software capability, while our product's hardware was unquestionably stronger. The President's response was, "Sounds to me like you have some loyalty issues. Would you be happier working for (competitor)?" The only sound heard after that was the hiss and static of dead air. The President ultimately got quite angry about the lack of contributions by the participants. He ended the conference by ordering us to each submit ideas via email. I know I played it very safe with my response. I'm sure he got very little of value in follow up."*

All three managers built walls with the doors to communication and idea-generation slammed shut. A leader must build a safe house for ideas and

growth. Offering an opinion or idea should get positive recognition. All three of these managers played the "bait and switch" game. They led employees to believe the environment was safe - "I want to hear your ideas." But as soon as an idea was offered, the idea and its creator were attacked. The true leader never plays the "bait and switch" game. When ideas are sought every employee is encouraged to participate. Creative thought must never bring criticism. In all three examples there could be "no bright ideas" because there was no safe room. Since employees were smart enough to keep their heads down and offered no new ideas, the whole company suffered. The employees were put in a no-win situation. The "bait and switch" game is worse than not asking for ideas and opinions in the first place. Employees can complain that no one asks for their input, but at least they are not tricked into believing their ideas might matter.

Action Ideas – Chapter Two

To minimize the damage caused by fear in the workplace:

- Provide employees an emotional "safe house."
- Admit your mistakes and adapt.
- Encourage and nurture the sharing of ideas.
- Recognize each opinion as having value.

3

"Steele" believes you never acknowledge the
importance of people who work for you.
In reality, you should:

Acknowledge the importance of people.

*"The deepest principle in human nature is the
craving to be appreciated."*
Dr. William James

Richard M. Highsmith

People need... not just want, but need... approval. This is a fundamental principle of human behavior. A three-year-old child demonstrates this fundamental principle of human behavior every time he utters the phrase, "Look what I can do," even when coloring on the walls. The child is saying, "Please approve of me and my creativity, Mom or Dad."

Renowned psychologist Frederick Herzberg's curiosity about the human need to feel "appreciated" and "approved of" at work, prompted him to study the work psyche. Herzberg found that pay and pleasant working conditions were important, but were clearly less important than feeling appreciated at work, and the nature of the work itself. According to Dr. Herzberg, mankind is not content with the satisfaction of lower-order needs at work—such as salary levels or safe and pleasant working conditions. Participants in the study reported they were more concerned with attaining the gratifying higher-level psychological needs of achievement, recognition, responsibility, advancement, and the

nature of the work itself.

We all need recognition to maximize our potential. Without it we become stagnant and dissatisfied with our work and lives. Theodore Roosevelt clearly defined a leader's role when he said, *"The best executive is the one who has sense enough to pick good men to do what he wants done, and self-restraint enough to keep from meddling with them while they do it."*

While I was teaching a leadership class, a young man named Dan gave me an excellent example of what happens when a manager is an opportunist, managing by intimidation, and stealing the positive light from his people.

"The issues we faced when completing the project were two- fold. First, my supervisor saw the possibility of failure and attempted to separate himself from the project. If the team failed, he could claim we acted without authority.

95

He never allowed any failure of the team to come back to him. Second, upon arriving on-site, we realized the planned location of the install would not support our client's requirements. The team sought approval from the client and installed the equipment in another location. The client made a big deal out of a job well done. Our supervisor claimed public credit but privately ripped in to the team, demeaning us, and claiming we had ignored his guidance. Even after our successes, he would not concede the fact that he was wrong in not trusting the engineers that he employed."

When Dan's manager separated himself from his team, he put himself in a safe room, but his whole team at risk. By not supporting his team, their professionalism and abilities, he robbed himself of any trust the team may have had for him and closed the door on communication.

Here is what a good leader would have done: When a competent team has a breakthrough idea and takes the risk of telling the client a proposed site is not appropriate, the leader should back them up. If they

get approval to make adjustments on their own, applaud their initiative. If their plan fails, a good leader steps in and helps solve the problem and searches for new ideas. When the client is pleased, the leader allows his team their moment in the spotlight. If a leader supports his team in this manner, future projects are bound to be easier for the team. They will respect the leader and each other and feel an incentive to find creative solutions to problems whenever they arise.

A colleague, who formerly worked in television news, shared with me how her manager's personal frustration in his own career track influenced his interaction with subordinates.

"An atypical day had me recording testimony, writing and editing the story of two people who kidnapped a biathlete, shot her and then killed her would- be rescuer. Next I had to drive like a woman possessed across the mountains to the feed point to do a live shot for the late news. Along the mountainous drive, a white tailed deer, seemed to fly out of the sky, crashing through

my windshield, sending shards of glass into my arm and neck. I lost control and the car careened down an embankment. I begged a farmer to shoot the badly injured deer and pull me back onto the road, which he did. I gunned the cracked up car over the mountains, mopped up my bleeding arm and neck, got to our sister station, handed off the tape, did the live shot and collapsed.

A more typical day followed. My news director suspended me for wrecking the car and then criticized me for sounding nasal during my live shot. A short time later I was working in a much larger market and my former news director was still intimidating and bullying every person unfortunate to be working for him"

Connie went to amazing measures to get the story on the air. Was she commended for her efforts? No. Was her extraordinary hard work acknowledged? No. Did this negatively affect her career? No. She moved up and he stayed behind. Good leaders do not intimidate and bully their subordinates.

The employee whom every business should want will seek satisfying work, leaders they can learn from, and companies that are moving in an exciting direction. They want to be part of the dream, the accomplishment.

The enthusiasm and creativity which positive employees bring with them is like breathing fresh air into a stale room. Their "oxygen" feeds growth and strengthens the company. Merle Crowell, author and historian, stated this eloquently; *"It's the men behind who 'make' the man ahead."* To recognize those "behind", a simple management principle works: **The effective manager gives credit to whom it's due.**

You don't need to carry pompoms and do cartwheels, but you do need to encourage, support, and mentor your employees. You are responsible for the morale of your department.

Bill, a current colleague shared an example of a leader who recognized this need.

>*"I taught in a private school where the Principal made it a routine to recognize positive things in his staff. There were annual reviews, pep talks and an end-of-year awards banquet where everyone was recognized for their efforts and some were given special recognition. One year I was awarded "Teacher of the Year" and that is something I won't soon forget. This was the lowest paid job I've held but the most rewarding in all other ways."*

Bill's final comment was the most telling. The meager balance in his checkbook seemed unimportant because a good leader frequently replenished Bill's "professional resource bank." Taking the time to acknowledge people's importance doesn't cost – it pays!

Action Ideas – Chapter Three

To value the importance of people in the workplace:

- Recognize all humans need approval.
- Catch people doing good work - being creative, developing new systems, building the team.
- Praise people for noteworthy behavior, thinking, and creativity.
- Turn perceived failures into learning opportunities.
- Smile more!

Richard M. Highsmith

4

"Steele" believes you give your opinion first, forcefully and often. In reality, good leaders:

Ask other people's opinions.

"I think we ought always to entertain our opinions with some measure of doubt. I shouldn't wish people dogmatically to believe any philosophy, not even mine. "

Bertrand Russell

Ask, then listen. Really listen. Tap the creativity and differing perspectives of all employees. An effective leader has learned that good ideas can come from anywhere and anyone. It may be the employee with years of experience who combines innovation with "tried and true" to get the job done. Or the "bright idea" might come from the newbie employee who offers a fresh solution to a nagging problem. If you treat all employees as creative wells of valuable information and ideas, they will continually shower you with great ideas and attitudes.

In some organizations all communication about change comes from the top down. (See Figure 1.) In this environment there is little lateral communication and virtually no rise of ideas from the base of the communication pyramid. This type of structure places an enormous burden on leadership. The "top few" must think of all possible ramifications of decisions. Any leader acting alone makes decisions from a limited viewpoint.

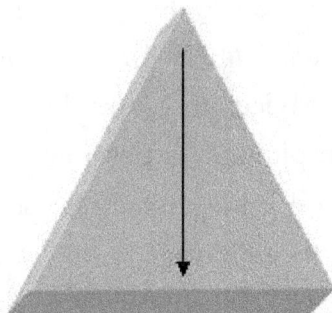

(Figure 1) Top Down Communication

Potential problem areas can be overlooked. In top-down communication, employees feel powerless to influence opinion. Since management does not invite employees to offer new ideas or solve problems, employees rarely "buy-in" to new plans. Without input and commitment from Jane and Joe, new plans soon become failed plans. And failed plans can widen the communication gap between managers and employees.

Creating a positive, productive work place

begins with open discussion. General Dwight D. Eisenhower once said, *"Communication is the art of getting someone else to do something you want done because he wants to do it."* Following General Eisenhower's advice, you should encourage the ideas of as many employees as possible. Communications will then flow in all directions through the organization. (See Figure 2.)

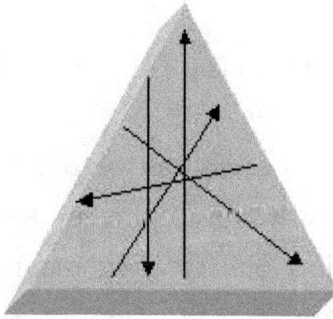

(Figure 2) Bee Hive Communication

When managers use the Bee Hive rather than top-down communication, employees are comfortable asking questions and offering creative ideas, which can lead to valuable solutions. If their ideas and suggestions are appreciated, they will feel more

ownership in the resulting change. Job satisfaction will soar. In this positive environment, employees will "try on" the proposed changes and feel confident suggesting ideas for improvement. This can happen naturally through conversations with each other and supervisors. Or a leader can schedule a meeting to initiate discussion and create a plan for change. Conducting effective meetings will be discussed later in this chapter.

I once worked with a woman, Ellie, who had been a part of an international charity. Her story aptly illustrates how detrimental poor communication could be to an organization... even one committed to humanitarian aid.

"My husband and I went to a remote Central American village for a two-year project with the promise of contact and support, only to hear absolutely nothing from the charity for nearly four months. When we had been there about six months, the charity sent a delegation of people to

visit the region and failed to inform us or involve us in any of the planning. We were informed a few days prior to the visit that we would be accompanying and translating for the group. Since we had no part in the planning, many of the areas where we had made the biggest difference weren't even visited.

After a year the decision was made to bring us home early. The charity didn't even send anyone to the town where we lived to see what the situation really was. We felt we had accomplished a great deal, but failure to involve us in the transition basically meant that all our work was for nothing. Without our involvement all the gains that had been made were lost."

Once Ellie and her husband arrived on site, they were left out of all planning and discussion. The delegation did not ask for details that would help it understand and appreciate the work of Ellie and her husband. Ultimately, they pulled the plug on the project.

The egos of management must never become more important than the project. Had the delegation involved Ellie in planning the visit, they would have had an opportunity to visit areas where real progress had been made. By seeking input from the staff on-site, they would have seen how donations from well wishing patrons were helping desperate villagers.

A minister at my church, Steve, told me about this experience while attending Seminary. It illustrates how encouraging open discussion can have a profound effect on the individual.

"I was attending school full time, working full time, married and a father of two pre-schoolers. As a result, I spent most of my time doing what I needed to do rather than doing what I wanted to do.

In a class on the Old Testament, one of the issues in the textbook piqued my curiosity, but the subject wasn't on the syllabus. I told the professor about the material that interested me. He suggested I do more research and write a

*paper. He said he would be very interested in
my thoughts. I told him with the limited time
available I could not pursue the regular
coursework and this additional task. He quickly
told me to forget other coursework and
concentrate on what interested me. I was
amazed! He went on to say students need
guidance in their learning, but when material
motivates someone they should be free to follow
its' direction. He allowed me to forego another
assignment and concentrate on the subject.*

*The opportunity changed my direction in
education and the way I approached learning
and even reading. This professor worked with
me to develop my strengths in areas that I would
never have explored if not for this incident. His
instruction was more than just teaching… it was
creative freedom."*

This is a terrific example of an effective leader.
He actively listened to his student. Steve described
the experience with this leader as "life changing."
Does this have application outside academia?
Absolutely! An exceptional leader asks questions and
thinks creatively about the response. Not every idea

is a great idea. But if a leader doesn't listen with an open mind that transforming, inspirational idea won't be heard.

A neighbor, Ann, told me about her experience with encouraging open discussion of ideas. She was working for a toy manufacturer at the time.

"I was working in Human Resources with three managers and seven employees like me. In this company, HR was involved with organizing yearly events like Halloween, employee soccer games, Christmas, fund raising, etc.

One year we had to plan the Christmas party with limited funds. The HR manager at the time set up a meeting for all the HR people to discuss options. She conducted a brainstorming session, which produced a great idea. We decided to hold the Christmas party IN the shop and transform it into a great event. It was quite challenging, as every supervisor in the shop had to be involved. We agreed to be very positive, as we were going to ask every employee to pitch in his or her ideas. Our goal was to make it a great, as well as, safe event. Since it was in the shop, we had to make sure everything was secured around the designated area. As planned, everybody was asked to actively participate, give ideas, and suggestions.

The party was a huge success partly because every employee felt like they were a part of a bigger thing! Even better than the party were the comments from many employees, "Someone cares about what I have to say!"

Ann's manager recognized the importance of involving as many employees as possible to creatively solve any potential problems. Encouraging supervisors and employees to participate produced an elegant, "employee-created" solution. The event was not only a "huge success," but employees felt empowered by their own "creative buzz." Were all the party ideas viable? No. Brainstorming is not about quality; it's about quantity. All ideas were thoughtfully considered. Ann and her team allowed everyone to participate, making acceptance by the group much more likely to occur.

Now that we have reviewed several examples regarding the importance of leaders asking other people's opinions, let's look at twelve steps to effectively manage a creative meeting:

1. <u>Have a clear purpose for the meeting.</u> Respect the time commitment of everyone. It's not just your schedule being affected.

2. <u>Have a written agenda.</u> Be realistic on the time required and the items needing attention. Distribute the agenda to all attendees several days before the meeting. This allows participants the opportunity to prepare their contribution.

3. <u>Follow the agenda.</u> Begin the meeting by telling everyone this is an "idea safe-house" and every member of the team and every idea will be valued. Assuming you have been realistic on the scheduled time, it important to take action on most if not all of the items.

4. <u>Tactfully keep the meeting moving forward.</u> When a team member goes off track, pull him or her back with the "parking lot" approach. You might say, "*Jim, that issue certainly deserves further discussion. Would you mind if we 'parked' it temporarily which would allow us to give it our full attention at another meeting?*"

5. <u>Show respect for all ideas.</u> Let everyone know you value his or her input, by listening. When seeking multiple ideas, record them on a flip chart or marker board. Help the group attack the problem, not each other.

6. <u>When brainstorming, the goal is quantity of ideas.</u> Initially the leader should step back, collect ideas and defer judgment. Creatively, there are no bad ideas. Every expressed thought could help move the group toward a solution.

7. <u>Positively acknowledge contributors.</u> Encourage more group participation with your body language: eye contact, nods, or smiles. Verbally motivate contributions by appreciative comments, such as "thank you."

8. <u>Try getting everyone's input.</u> Draw out any shy participants or late arrivals. People are more likely to support what they help create. Participants may hitchhike a more defined solution on someone else's creative thought. In an "idea safe" atmosphere, the magic of creativity flourishes, settling on the shoulders of all involved.

9. <u>Spend less time talking about the problem.</u> Let participants know the idea generation is limited to 10 minutes. The leader should allow this process to play itself out. The group is then asked to begin evaluating the possible solutions. Again, it is important for the leader to allow the group to make the judgments while controlling any negative feedback.

Spend more time working on the possible solution and the plan to achieve it.

10. <u>Share the floor during the meeting.</u> You want a   dialogue with many, not a monologue of one.   The leader might prompt additional creative input by asking questions.   For example, "What effect could this solution have on other departments?" or "How could we diffuse that cost?"

11. <u>Distribute authority and responsibility.</u> When the group has selected the most effective idea, work on specific steps toward implementation. The plan evolving from this group effort will be more likely to have examined the issue from multiple sides.   It will also have broader support and a much higher likelihood of success.   Allow several people to be part of the implementation.   Make a note of who is responsible for what.

12. Start and stop on time. Show consideration for everyone's busy schedule. For every minute you delay or go over the allotted time you can subtract two minutes of morale.

Asking opinions isn't only a leadership tool, it is essential in team building. A popular concept currently making the management training circuit is that organizations tend to form "silos." Departments and individuals focus on their own projects with little to no understanding about what other departments are doing. This process creates isolation. When a problem develops, it can be compounded by each group staying in its respective silo. A former colleague, Al, cites an example of a silo.

> *"A customer was experiencing a series of intermittent system failures that resulted in interruption of business transactions. The problem kept occurring and, each time, a local service representative replaced a suspected defective component. Our branch office failed to properly involve product support resources. On the fifth occurrence, the customer was irate and*

demanded a complete and total resolution. The local branch finally asked for a product support engineer to be brought in. He readily found the problem and replicated the error to "prove" the culprit module had, indeed, been identified. The client lost confidence in the local office. Had support been involved in the call earlier, the customer would have perceived the local office as professionally managing the situation. But their "turf" issue proliferated a relationship issue that existed between the local office and the support group for some months."

A leader can break through the silos by asking opinions from his subordinates and people from other departments affected by the issue. In this study the local office endangered the relationship with the client by refusing to ask for opinions outside their silo. Product support resources were not immediately coordinated to resolve the problem. The local office had developed an "us" versus "them" mentality. As a

result, the customer experienced five outages of service. The "team" is the whole company working together to meet customer needs. Remember, asking other people's opinions is a team building principle as well.

Action Ideas - Chapter Four

To maximize other peoples' opinions:

- Enthusiastically ask for input and new ideas.
- Actively listen to each person.
- Encourage the expression of new ideas and approaches.
- Involve as many employees as possible in planning change.
- Manage better meetings by following the Creative Meeting Steps

5

"Steele" believes you should keep people busy.
In reality, a leader will:

Be a Macro Manager.

*"When Alexander the Great visited Diogenes and asked
whether he could do anything for the famed teacher,
Diogenes replied: 'Only stand out of my light.' Perhaps
some day we shall know how to heighten creativity. Until
then, one of the best things we can do for creative men and
women is to stand out of their light."*
John W. Gardner

Shine the light on creativity. Let the creative process work. Clearly define the goals and objectives. Give your employees support and freedom to reach those goals and then *get out of their light.* In this environment, team members will feel empowered to create new ideas and find creative solutions to old problems. Potential roadblocks will be anticipated and alternative routes quickly planned. Allowing a free-flow approach to work produces powerful enterprise – not *busy work.*

A former colleague, Sarah, at one time worked for city government. She told me a remarkable tale of appearance being more important than results.

"Shortly after I began work, I noticed many staff members kept enormous stacks of papers and file folders all over their desk and floor. In many cases it was impossible to tell where one job began and the other ended. All of my assignments were organized in a file cabinet by

priority. I only had the necessary Items on my desk that required my full attention because I don't like clutter.

After two or three months I was called into my superior's office. He said I did not seem to have enough work to do since my desk was virtually empty. I pulled out my log which tracked all projects I had been assigned and completed. I went on to explain to him that I chose not to have all of my files on my desk because this shows a lack of professionalism. He refused to recognize the work that I had accomplished and reprimanded me for not staying busy. The next morning I stacked folders, manuals, and papers all over my desk and on the floor. I put post-it notes on my computer and desk. No one ever bothered me again regarding my workload."

This is a classic example of micromanagement. Sarah's boss didn't like employees to stand out or look like they were not part of his "work model." He clung to arbitrary, pre-established norms that went beyond performance. He was more concerned that Sarah *looked like* she was *busy* than he was about the quality or amount of work she actually accomplished.

People work in different ways. Sarah prefers order and neatness. An effective leader focuses on outcome and productivity, not individual work habits. Simply *looking busy* is meaningless. When meeting with an employee to discuss performance, allow him or her to explain how they plan to meet deadlines and accomplish tasks.

Some managers agree to try a different system or change a way to handle a problem. However, their words are hollow. Craig, a colleague, is an ordained minister. As you will see from his prior experience, sometimes it's not only about keeping people *busy*, it is also about using deception to manage potential problems, creating the illusion of change and flexibility.

"There had been a steady decline in membership and charitable contributions over several years. The Board of Directors was given a mandate to change things. I was hired as a Director to focus on pastor and church services and to facilitate change. I worked with pastors having problems, with churches that did not have

pastors, and as a resource person for both pastors and churches. The general morale of the pastors, churches and districts immediately responded and things were going well.

My position was the first of several announced changes to be made at the denominational level. As I traveled, I talked about other changes on the horizon. Ultimately a problem developed because no other changes were taking place. I was becoming a PR person who was to trying to keep people happy with expected change, when in fact there would be no other changes. I explained to different Board members that people trusted me and if the announced changes weren't Forthcomin there would be a large slip in morale. I let them know if no action was taken by the end of the year, I would submit my resignation.

The consensus of the Board was that it was easier to let one person go than to manage the change. I was gone before New Year's Eve. The denomination continues to decline and has recently sold its general offices and college properties to offset the continued decline in contributions."

Management can be downright hard at times. With a myriad of problems coming out of the telephone and leaking from the computer onto the desk, a bunch of promised changes may seem like a great idea to stave off unrest. Craig's experience demonstrates how a little deception can defraud a whole team. It was easy. *Promise* changes, but never actually *make* the changes. This is at best a temporary fix. Broken promises can only be explained away for a short time. Work relationships are like checking accounts. Each broken promise debits the Bank of Management Trust. A leader maintains a positive balance in the account by keeping his or her promises, no matter how small. Craig refused to run a negative balance and moved on with his life.

Team members can also be guilty of mistaking busy activity for results. Another former colleague, Annie, discovered it isn't always a boss who squishes creativity by standing in the way of progress.

I was responsible for creating direct marketing

programs for a large technology corporation. The marketing and sales functions were separate in this organization. I was assigned to a sales team that was driven to reporting activity in accounts even when it added no value to the sales process. They were literally stuck in a rut of being activity-rich and results-poor! They had great products to offer but were perplexed as to why sales were falling. It seemed to me there was a poor connection between the efforts of the previous marketing person and the sales team.

The challenge I faced with this account team was to refocus their energy and instill confidence with a better way to market to their customers Our first mailer was a brief request for feedback on what key factors moved the customer to buy from us. We very quickly improved understanding of our customer and directly attributed the correlation between orders received and each marketing effort targeted at the account. The relationship between marketing and sales turned around. The customer saw concrete examples of 'partnering' with the sales team, showing our team was clearly focused on solving their business problems. Eventually, it was common

to hear one of the sales team members comment to the customer, 'I will run that by my marketing team and get back to you with a proposal.'"

Annie's description of the problem, "activity-rich and results-poor," illustrates the trap team members can fall into without clearly- defined goals and objectives. Annie was able to creatively step "out of the box," gather information for establishing goals and objectives, and lay it all out for the sales department. The sales department quickly grasped how this new creative thinking could help them retain old accounts and create new ones.

There are times when goals seem clearly defined, yet little progress is actually being made on a project. A creative manager can step in and work with the group to explore the cause and effect of current lack-luster efforts. This should be done in a non-

confrontational manner, allowing each member to offer ideas, ponder results, and help find solutions.

I once owned a medium-sized manufacturing company that supplied the hospitality industry with framed art. We were having some serious issues with shipping finished artwork to clients. We used large cardboard boxes on wooden pallets. Damaged product was a common occurrence but nobody seemed able to think of a way to solve the problem. We had tried multiple ways of packing, many different types of protective wrapping and various strapping techniques.

Finally in frustration I presented the problem in an open staff meeting. A nineteen-year-old employee who had been working for me about three weeks asked a simple question, *"How much do the boxes, pallets and protective wrapping cost? "* The teenager then came up with a solution that was elegant in it's simplicity. He said, *"Gosh, for that much money we could build wooden crates."* We were lost in the forest; he saw the tree!

Mary, a former teacher, told me a story of "great ideas" that can be robbed of value by busy work and not anticipating a roadblock.

"I taught in a private school where the upper grades were encouraged to interact with the lower grades academically. This helped the older students learn the material well in order to teach it to the younger kids. The younger students listened and responded to the older students, so the situation was valid and useful as an educational method.

I teamed up with a lower schoolteacher to have my high-schoolers work with her kids on some science lessons. After the lesson had been taught, the 'higher, faster' learners would move on to separate stations with a team of high schoolers. A second team of high schoolers would work with the younger kids who still needed to master the original content. The faster learners were assigned additional materials, which kept the first group occupied while the 'slower kids' caught up. The unfortunate outcome was that all the students (elementary and high school) in the 'fast group' would dally

over the additional materials because they knew the more they finished, the more uninteresting, unimaginative 'busy work' would be assigned to them. There was no real reward to mastering the content at a faster pace."

Mary's example could happen in any work place. One bright employee has a great idea. The group enthusiasm gives the project a "Go!" before examining potential roadblocks. A great leader will allow what I call "creative incubation." You must allow time for an idea to fully develop. Make sure the idea is ready before introducing   it into the workplace.

The ubiquitous Post-it® Notes is a great example of giving a creative idea time to work its way to success. Post-it® Notes, as we know it today, was not the planned product. Spencer Silver was working in the 3M research laboratories trying to find a strong adhesive. Silver developed a new adhesive, but it was even weaker than what 3M already manufactured. It stuck to objects, but could easily be lifted off.   His supervisor did not squish Silver's

creation. In fact, management spread information about the discovery to other scientists working at 3M. Another scientist, Arthur Fry, used Silver's adhesive to coat page markers. With the weak adhesive, the page markers stayed in place, yet lifted off without damaging the paper pages.

3M began distributing Post-it ® Notes nationwide in 1980. The communication of creative ideas was encouraged at 3M and the result is one of the most popular office products available today.

A wise leader allows originality and creativity to flourish by focusing on goals and objectives – not the niggling details. Set the parameters and allow people to flex their innovation muscles. Remember, creativity comes willingly from team members who feel appreciated and valued. Inspire your team by being an openly supportive macro manager.

Action Ideas – Chapter Five

To become a Macro Manager:

- Create a "safe house" environment and let the creative process work.
- Incubate ideas until they are strong enough to survive.
- Clearly define goals and give your employees breathing room.
- Be open to different work styles.
- Practice rigorous honesty and deliver on promises.
- Encourage "creative work" not "busy work," and anticipate roadblocks.

6

CONCLUSION

"The employer generally gets the employees he deserves."
Sir Walter Gilbey, English Author and Philanthropist

The ideas discussed in this book are rooted in the desire to help you become a better manager. Building a safe house for creative thought, encouraging and nurturing individuals' ideas will create a better work place for you and those who work for you. Employees temperaments come in many sizes and shapes. Their workplace needs and desires often change with their life stages. A "one size fits all" management style squishes creativity. Look at the individual, consider the problem, and examine the possibilities. Then personalize your approach. How do you know which strategy to use on whom and when? Look to yourself for the answers. Employ <u>your</u> talent, enriched by personal learning and experience. Exercise some of your own creativity. Be willing to take some risks and try different approaches.

If you want to <u>be</u> the leader who takes your company to the next level, maintain your focus on the creative ideas and needs of your employees. Valuable employees do not do their best work based primarily on how much they are paid. More often it is the respect they receive and their sense of being a part of something important.

Do you foster, value, and protect new ideas? Encourage open discussion of ideas and acknowledge the importance of each idea and each "idea creator." Ask for input and opinion. Give your employees the freedom to creatively pursue company goals.

You can be the catalyst for transforming a business environment. You can be the leader your people will not only want to follow, but want to *be like*. The steps to a productive and idea driven work environment are simple and straightforward. Implementing them takes courage, diligence and a willingness to continually reexamine each situation, each challenge and most of all - **yourself**.

Inspire your team. Build a safe house for ideas. Nurture both the *idea* and the employee. Shine a light on the idea and the "idea creator."

"Remember: Don't Squish Creativity."

Richard M. Highsmith

About the Author

Rick is a sought after trainer and speaker for Fortune 500 companies. His messages focus on the value of collaboration and on how dynamic, creative communication improves team effectiveness. Rick has been a guest lecturer at Harvard Business School, has trained officers of an international cruise ship line, and worked throughout the U.S., Canada and Europe. Having studied improvisational comedy for one year, Rick recognizes how humor enhances the learning experience.

Rick has a Masters Degree in Clinical Psychology. His background as a Mental Health Counselor gives him tremendous insight into how to motivate and inspire people using positive reinforcement. Additionally he has built and sold two successful businesses in the past 25 years, so he understands the challenges of leadership and management from practical experience.

Rick's passion is family. Donna, his wife, reader and editor of his writing, best friend and biggest supporter, has stood by every challenge and endeavor for the last thirty-six years. Their adult son, and daughter-in-law blessed them with three precocious, precious grandchildren. A close second on the passion scale is scuba diving and boating. The family recently rented a house in Key Largo to celebrate his son's birthday. Laughing with family, doting on grandkids, AND daily diving opportunities, made Rick a believer in nirvana!

NOTES

<u>NOTES</u>

<u>NOTES</u>

<u>NOTES</u>

www.ingramcontent.com/pod-product-compliance
Lightning Source LLC
LaVergne TN
LVHW021504080426
835509LV00018B/2395